MW00942627

# Becoming a Peculiar Person in Christ

## Working God's Principles

The Reverend James A. Tazewell

Cover Image and Author Image by Angela Baker Ward.



WestBow Press books may be ordered through booksellers or by contacting:

WestBow Press
A Division of Thomas Nelson & Zondervan
1663 Liberty Drive
Bloomington, IN 47403
www.westbowpress.com
1 (866) 928-1240



All Scripture quotations are taken from the King James Version.

ISBN: 978-1-9736-9656-8 (sc)
ISBN: 978-1-9736-9658-2 (hc)
ISBN: 978-1-9736-9657-5 (e)

Library of Congress Control Number: 2020912882

Print information available on the last page.

WestBow Press rev. date: 07/21/2020

# The Dedication Prayer

I pray to my God, the Father of heaven and earth, in Jesus Christ's name, for His blessing upon this book. Lord, I ask that you cover this book in your shed blood, and that you will cause every word written on these pages to influence all who read them and that they will hear your voice only through these words. And Lord, my prayer is that all men will be saved according to your desire for creation, according to your salvation plan in Jesus Christ, my Lord and Savior. I pray that you will anoint every chapter with your Holy anointing and cause an awakening in the souls of every

---

*"Now unto Him that is able to keep you from falling, and to present you faultless before the presence of His glory with exceeding joy, to the only wise God our Savior, be glory and majesty, dominion and power, both now and forever. Amen" (Jude 1:24–25).*

reader and believer who obtains this book. I pray that all minds will be bound to the will of God in Christ Jesus and that every heart will be submissive and humble to the obtaining of God's purpose in their lives.

I pray that men, women, and children who read this book will change their perspective of who you are in the Holy Scriptures and realize that you are a Holy, longsuffering God who is full of compassion, unconditional love, and mercy, and that as a Holy God, you do not commune with sin or accept evil and wickedness in your presence. Therefore, God, my prayer is that every heart will be taken captive and every life that desires your salvation will become peculiar according to your Holy Word in Christ Jesus.

---

*"Now unto Him that is able to keep you from falling, and to present you faultless before the presence of His glory with exceeding joy, to the only wise God our Savior, be glory and majesty, dominion and power, both now and forever. Amen" (Jude 1:24–25).*

I pray that the Holy Bible will once again be a compass for everyone who desires to follow Christ Jesus, pointing them toward the righteousness of the eternal kingdom in heaven. Heavenly Father, I pray that your will will be done in Jesus Christ's name. Amen!

---

*"Now unto Him that is able to keep you from falling, and to present you faultless before the presence of His glory with exceeding joy, to the only wise God our Savior, be glory and majesty, dominion and power, both now and forever. Amen" (Jude 1:24–25).*

# Introduction

Without the new birth, we cannot see the kingdom of God or receive eternal life and salvation through Jesus Christ. Neither will we be able to enter the kingdom of God. To receive this life, we must repent of our sins to God and believe in the Lord Jesus Christ. It is impossible for us, of ourselves, to escape the pit of sin in which we are sunk. Our hearts are evil, and we cannot change that. "Who can bring a clean thing out of an unclean?" (Job 14:4). No one, and the fleshly mind will not adhere to the things of God or set

---

*"Now unto Him that is able to keep you from falling, and to present you faultless before the presence of His glory with exceeding joy, to the only wise God our Savior, be glory and majesty, dominion and power, both now and forever. Amen" (Jude 1:24–25).*

itself to please God. Unbelievers cannot and will not mingle with the things of God in Christ.

Know this, that there is no true excellence of character apart from God, and the only way to Him is Christ Jesus, the One who came in the way and, when He came of age, taught the way. Then, at the appointed hour of His life, He sacrificed Himself according to the way, showing the world that the heart of God the Father yearns over His earthly children with a love stronger than death. In giving up His only begotten Son, He has poured out to us all of heaven in one gift. It is an eternal fact that God loves us with an everlasting love that cannot be fathomed. His love is so boundless that it can be known only by faith in Him. God gave His only Son to be made sin for us, that we might be made the righteousness of God in Him. Jesus Christ was

---

*"Now unto Him that is able to keep you from falling, and to present you faultless before the presence of His glory with exceeding joy, to the only wise God our Savior, be glory and majesty, dominion and power, both now and forever. Amen" (Jude 1:24–25).*

made into that which God hates—sin—that we might be made into that which God loves—righteousness.

Shall we not regard the mercy of God? What more could He have done? Let us place ourselves in right relation to Him who has loved us with amazing love. Let us avail ourselves of the means provided for us, that we may be transformed into His likeness and restored to fellowship with the ministering angels to harmony and communion with the Father and the Son. How shall a man be just with God? How shall the sinner be made righteous? It is only through Christ Jesus that we can be brought into harmony with God and holiness, but how are we to come to Christ Jesus? Come just as you are: brokenhearted, captive, locked up and bound, grief stricken, sorrowful, afflicted, wounded, bruised, hurting, and sin filled. For Jesus said, according to Matthew 11:28–30, "Come unto me, all ye that labor and are heavy laden,

---

*"Now unto Him that is able to keep you from falling, and to present you faultless before the presence of His glory with exceeding joy, to the only wise God our Savior, be glory and majesty, dominion and power, both now and forever. Amen" (Jude 1:24–25).*

and I will give you rest. Take my yoke upon you, and learn of me; for I am meek and lowly in heart: and ye shall find rest unto your souls, for my yoke is easy and my burden is light."

The virtue that goes forth from Christ Jesus leads to genuine repentance. Jesus is the source of every right impulse, the only one who can implant in the heart enmity against sin. Every desire for truth and purity, every conviction of our own sinfulness, is evidence that His Spirit is moving upon our hearts. Jesus Christ must be revealed to us as the Savior, dying for the sins of the world. As we behold the Lamb of God upon the cross of Calvary, the mystery of redemption begins to unfold to our minds and the goodness of God leads us to repentance. In dying for us, Christ manifested a love that is incomprehensible, and as we behold this love, it softens the heart, impresses the mind, and inspires contrition in the soul.

---

*"Now unto Him that is able to keep you from falling, and to present you faultless before the presence of His glory with exceeding joy, to the only wise God our Savior, be glory and majesty, dominion and power, both now and forever. Amen" (Jude 1:24–25).*

As Christ draws us to look upon His cross, to behold Him whom our sins have pierced, the commandment comes home to the conscience: "Repent: for the kingdom of heaven is at hand" (Matthew 4:17b). Repentance includes sorrow for sin and turning away from it. We will not renounce sin unless we see its sinfulness, and until we turn completely from it in heart, there will be no real change in our lives. Many Christians fail to understand the true nature of repentance. We sorrow that we have sinned and even make an outward reformation, because we fear that our wrongdoing will bring us suffering, but this is not repentance.

When our hearts yield to the influence of the Spirit of God, our consciences will be quickened, and as sinners, we will discern something of the depth and sacredness of God's Holy Law, the foundation of His government in heaven and on the earth. The light that lights up everyone

---

*"Now unto Him that is able to keep you from falling, and to present you faultless before the presence of His glory with exceeding joy, to the only wise God our Savior, be glory and majesty, dominion and power, both now and forever. Amen" (Jude 1:24–25).*

who comes into the world (John 1:9) illumines the secret chambers of our souls, and the hidden things of darkness are made manifest. Conviction takes hold of our minds and hearts, and as sinners, we have a sense of the righteousness of God and feel the terror of appearing in our own guilt and uncleanness before the "searcher of hearts" (Psalm 139:23-24). We see the love of God, the beauty of holiness, and the joy of purity, and we long to be cleansed and restored to communion with heaven.

The Bible says, "Blessed is he whose transgression is forgiven, whose sin is covered. Blessed is the man unto whom the Lord imputeth not iniquity, and in whose spirit there is no guile" (Psalm 32:1–2). The Spirit of God is pleading with us to seek the only things that can give us peace and rest—the grace of Christ Jesus and the joy of holiness. Through influences seen and unseen, our Savior is constantly at work

---

*"Now unto Him that is able to keep you from falling, and to present you faultless before the presence of His glory with exceeding joy, to the only wise God our Savior, be glory and majesty, dominion and power, both now and forever. Amen" (Jude 1:24–25).*

to draw our minds away from the unsatisfying pleasures of sin to the infinite blessings that may be ours in Him.

To all of humanity, vainly seeking to drink from the broken cisterns of this world, the divine message is addressed: "Let him that is athirst come. And whosoever will, let him take the water of life freely" (Revelation 22:17). The water of life is a symbol of God in Christ as the Spirit, flowing into His redeemed people to supply their lives. God offers us free nourishment that feeds our soul. How do we get it? We are to come, listen, seek, and call upon Him. God's salvation is freely offered, but it cannot nourish our souls unless we eagerly receive it. We can't receive salvation by living a better life, but only by being spiritually reborn.

Without the new birth, we cannot see the kingdom of God (John 3:3) or receive eternal life and salvation through Jesus Christ. The new birth is a recreating and transformation

---

*"Now unto Him that is able to keep you from falling, and to present you faultless before the presence of His glory with exceeding joy, to the only wise God our Savior, be glory and majesty, dominion and power, both now and forever. Amen" (Jude 1:24–25).*

by God through the Holy Spirit. Through this process, eternal life from God Himself is imparted to believers, who then become children of God and new people. We should no longer live according to this world, but by the Word of God to the changing of our lives, because through Christ and the indwelling Holy Spirit, we are created after God in righteousness and true holiness.

The new birth is necessary, because apart from Christ, all people, by our inherent natures, are sinners, incapable of obeying and pleasing God. Salvation comes to those who repent of their sin, turn to God, and place personal faith in Jesus Christ as Lord and Savior. It involves a transition from an old life of sin to a new life of obedience to God in Jesus Christ. If we are truly born again, we're set free from the bondage of sin and receive a spiritual desire and disposition to obey God and follow the leading of the Holy Spirit.

---

*"Now unto Him that is able to keep you from falling, and to present you faultless before the presence of His glory with exceeding joy, to the only wise God our Savior, be glory and majesty, dominion and power, both now and forever. Amen" (Jude 1:24–25).*

Romans 8:1 says, "There is therefore now no condemnation to them which are in Christ Jesus, who walk not after the flesh, but after the Spirit."

After being born again, we should live righteous lives, love unconditionally, avoid a life of sin, and by all means not love the world or the things of it. After being born of God, we cannot make sin a habitual practice in our lives. We should live each day as children of God with a sincere desire and victorious endeavor to please Him and avoid all evil. This comes only through the love given to us by Jesus Christ in a sustained relationship with Him, and through dependence on His Word with the guidance of the Holy Spirit. And we no more address the ideas of the fleshly mind, but now live our lives under the guise of the Holy Spirit.

As proclaimed believers, if we continue to live as unconverted sinners, then eternal death will be our demise.

---

*"Now unto Him that is able to keep you from falling, and to present you faultless before the presence of His glory with exceeding joy, to the only wise God our Savior, be glory and majesty, dominion and power, both now and forever. Amen" (Jude 1:24–25).*

Just as we can be born of the Spirit by receiving the life of God, we can also extinguish that life by ungodly choices and unrighteous living, and thus die spiritually. Scripture concurs: "If you live after the flesh, you shall die" (Romans 8:13). "For the wages of sin in the flesh is death; but the gift of God is eternal life through Jesus Christ our Lord" (Romans 6:23). The Holy Spirit is the sustainer of that life, and He has been made available to all who believe in and receive Jesus Christ into our lives.

Without the Holy Spirit, we cannot belong to Jesus Christ and be united with Him, nor can we become God's adopted children. The Spirit is the power of our new lives, a lifelong process of change making us more like Christ. When we receive Christ by faith, we begin an immediate personal relationship with God. The Holy Spirit works in us to help us become who God predestined us to become in Christ Jesus.

---

*"Now unto Him that is able to keep you from falling, and to present you faultless before the presence of His glory with exceeding joy, to the only wise God our Savior, be glory and majesty, dominion and power, both now and forever. Amen" (Jude 1:24–25).*

The power we receive from the Holy Spirit gives us courage, boldness, confidence, insight, ability, and authority, and we need all these to fulfill our God-given mission on earth. This power is not some impersonal force, but a manifestation of the Holy Spirit by which the presence, glory, and works of Jesus are present with His people.

Other results of our power through the Holy Spirit include prophetic utterances and praise, enhanced sensitivity to sin that grieves the Holy Spirit, a greater seeking after righteousness that conforms to Christ, and a deeper awareness of God's judgment against all ungodliness. There also is a manifestation of the various gifts of the Holy Spirit, including the word of wisdom, the word of knowledge, faith, gifts of healing, the working of miracles, prophecy, discerning of spirits, various kinds of tongues, and interpretation of tongues. These gifts are noted in 1 Corinthians 12:8–10.

---

*"Now unto Him that is able to keep you from falling, and to present you faultless before the presence of His glory with exceeding joy, to the only wise God our Savior, be glory and majesty, dominion and power, both now and forever. Amen" (Jude 1:24–25).*

This power of the Holy Spirit is sustained in believers' lives by prayer, witness, worship in the Spirit, and sanctified living. However powerful the initial coming of the Holy Spirit upon believers may be, if it does not find expression in a life of prayer, witness, and holiness, the experience will fade. Prayer is the necessary link to receiving God's blessings and power, and the fulfillment of His promises. At our conversion, we receive the Holy Spirit as a seal to our salvation in God through Christ. As we persist in our walk with Christ through God's Word, we build the Holy Spirit within us, and He releases the power of life through us to become overcomers, victors, and bold disciples of Jesus.

As believers, we must live by the Word of God and call to Him through prayer. In some respects, God has limited Himself to the holy, believing, persevering prayers of His people, and many things will not be accomplished in God's

---

*"Now unto Him that is able to keep you from falling, and to present you faultless before the presence of His glory with exceeding joy, to the only wise God our Savior, be glory and majesty, dominion and power, both now and forever. Amen" (Jude 1:24–25).*

kingdom without the intercessory prayers of believers. For example, God desires to send workers into the gospel harvest, and Jesus Christ teaches that this will be fully accomplished only through the prayers of His people: "Pray ye therefore the Lord of the harvest, that He will send forth laborers into the harvest" (Matthew 9:38). God's power to accomplish many of His purposes is released only through the earnest and effectual prayers of His people on behalf of the progress of His kingdom. If we fail to pray, we may actually be hindering the accomplishment of God's redemptive purpose, both for ourselves individually and for the church as a body.

Prayer can be effective only if it is done according to the perfect will of God. So while you're praying and whatever you're praying for, say, "Thy will be done in earth, as it is in heaven," in Jesus's name (Matthew 6:10). Amen! Through a life of unceasing prayer, we become great witnesses by the

---

*"Now unto Him that is able to keep you from falling, and to present you faultless before the presence of His glory with exceeding joy, to the only wise God our Savior, be glory and majesty, dominion and power, both now and forever. Amen" (Jude 1:24–25).*

Holy Spirit. We receive power to witness for Christ and work effectively within the Church and before the world. We receive the same anointing that descended upon Christ and the disciples, enabling us to proclaim God's Word and work miracles.

God's intent is for all Christians to experience baptism in the Holy Spirit, which gives spiritual gifts to individual members with which to edify or strengthen the Church. These gifts are a manifestation of the Spirit through individuals by which Christ's presence, love, truth, and righteous standards are made real to the fellowship of believers for the common good. Also, the Spirit makes us holy and consecrated, separate from the world, and set apart from sin so that we may have close fellowship with God and serve Him.

Holiness is a work of both God and His people. To accomplish God's will, believers must respond to the

---

*"Now unto Him that is able to keep you from falling, and to present you faultless before the presence of His glory with exceeding joy, to the only wise God our Savior, be glory and majesty, dominion and power, both now and forever. Amen" (Jude 1:24–25).*

sanctifying work of the Holy Spirit by ceasing to do evil, cleansing ourselves "from all filthiness of the flesh and spirit" (2 Corinthians 7:1), and keeping ourselves unspotted from the world. The purpose of separation is that as God's people, we might persevere in salvation, faith, and holiness, living wholly for God as our Lord and Father. If we separate ourselves properly, God will reward us by drawing near with His protection, blessing, and Fatherly care. He promises to be everything that a good father should be—our counselor and guide, loving and cherishing us as His own children. As newborn believers, let us hold on to God's strong hands in Christ Jesus, our Lord and Savior, for our lives are now hidden in Christ. Amen and amen.

Welcome to the Body of Christ. As you read this book, you will begin to understand what Jesus meant when He said, "[I]f any man desire to come after me let him deny

---

*"Now unto Him that is able to keep you from falling, and to present you faultless before the presence of His glory with exceeding joy, to the only wise God our Savior, be glory and majesty, dominion and power, both now and forever. Amen" (Jude 1:24–25).*

himself; pick up his cross and follow me. For whosoever will save his life shall lose it; but whosoever shall lose his life for my sake and the gospel's, the same shall save it" (Mark 8:34–35). As a minister of God in Christ Jesus, I pray that the Body of Christ will begin to follow Jesus's word and know what it means to live abundantly right now and have eternal life as well.

God has spoken in the beginning as He also speaks even now: "But the word is very nigh unto thee, even in thy mouth, and in thy heart, that thou mayest do it. See I have set before thee this day life, and good, and death and evil; In that I command thee this day to love the Lord thy God, to walk in His ways, and to keep His commandments and His statutes and His judgments, that thou mayest live and multiply: and the Lord thy God shall bless thee in the land whither thou goest to possess it" (Deuteronomy 30:14–16).

---

*"Now unto Him that is able to keep you from falling, and to present you faultless before the presence of His glory with exceeding joy, to the only wise God our Savior, be glory and majesty, dominion and power, both now and forever. Amen" (Jude 1:24–25).*

God has called you to obey His commandments while reminding you that His laws are not hidden or beyond your reach. Obeying God is reasonable, sensible, and beneficial, and the most difficult part is simply deciding to start. God bless you in your walk with Him.

"I write so that you may know how you ought to conduct yourself in … the church of the living God, the pillar and ground of the truth" (1 Timothy 3:15). God the Father—through Jesus Christ, the Holy Spirit, and the apostles—has given you guidelines for living in and being part of the kingdom of heaven. But to advance in this new life that God has given you, you must follow His every command without any doubt, for now you walk by faith and not by sight. God has also given you all things that pertain to life and godliness. Therefore humble yourself, pray, seek His face, and

---

*"Now unto Him that is able to keep you from falling, and to present you faultless before the presence of His glory with exceeding joy, to the only wise God our Savior, be glory and majesty, dominion and power, both now and forever. Amen" (Jude 1:24–25).*

turn from your wicked ways, that the Lord your God may hear from heaven and heal your land (2 Chronicles 7:14).

“Humble yourselves therefore under the mighty hand of God, that He may exalt you in due time: Casting all your care upon Him; for He careth for you” (1 Peter 5:6–7). Are you faced with the troubles of this life continually, day in and day out, worried, and weighed down with burdens that only Christ Jesus can remove? He knows from experience the weaknesses of humanity. The Bible says, “The Lord hath laid on Him the iniquity of us all. He was oppressed, and He was afflicted, yet He opened not His mouth: He is brought as a lamb to the slaughter, and as a sheep before her shearers is dumb, so He openeth not His mouth” (Isaiah 53:6b–7). Christ Jesus “was in all points tempted like as we are, yet without sin” (Hebrews 4:15b).

“Surely he hath borne our griefs, and carried our sorrows:

---

*“Now unto Him that is able to keep you from falling, and to present you faultless before the presence of His glory with exceeding joy, to the only wise God our Savior, be glory and majesty, dominion and power, both now and forever. Amen” (Jude 1:24–25).*

yet we did esteem Him stricken, smitten of God, and afflicted. But he was wounded for our transgressions, He was bruised for our iniquities: the chastisement of our peace was upon Him: and with His stripes we are healed" (Isaiah 53:4–5). Just look back a few pages into the Book and witness the bloody figure at the whipping post. Now look at your life and understand that you played a part in that brutal beating of the Creator of heaven and earth, who's now the Savior of the world. We weren't more powerful than Jesus, but He humbled Himself to a sinner's death, "even the death of the cross" (Philippians 2:8b).

After carefully looking into the Book and listening to the Word as I read, I've come to understand that Jesus Christ did not die for the sake of dying, but for the sake of what He created. The Bible says, "All things were made by Him; and

---

*"Now unto Him that is able to keep you from falling, and to present you faultless before the presence of His glory with exceeding joy, to the only wise God our Savior, be glory and majesty, dominion and power, both now and forever. Amen" (Jude 1:24–25).*

without Him was not anything made that was made. In Him was life; and the life was the light of men" (John 1:3–4).

Here we see the mystery that God desired to express Himself in rare form through man: "Let us make man in our image, after our likeness: So God created man in His own image, in the image of God created He him; male and female created He them" (Genesis 1:26–27). We were created not merely to contain food in our stomach or knowledge in our mind, but to contain God in our spirit. But before we could receive God as life into our spirit, sin entered us, made us enemies of God, and transmuted our bodies into sinful flesh. The Bible says, "And the eyes of them both were opened, and they knew that they were naked; and they sewed fig leaves together, and made themselves aprons; and hid themselves from the presence of the Lord God amongst the trees of the garden" (Genesis 3:7–8).

---

*"Now unto Him that is able to keep you from falling, and to present you faultless before the presence of His glory with exceeding joy, to the only wise God our Savior, be glory and majesty, dominion and power, both now and forever. Amen" (Jude 1:24–25).*

To this very day, without the true knowledge of Christ Jesus in God, through the power and presence of the Holy Spirit, we still hide ourselves because of our inner nakedness. The voice of the Lord God walks through the land in the cool of this day, calling our names and asking, "Where art thou?" And we ignore Him and fail to acknowledge Him: "I heard thy voice in this day, and I was afraid, because I was naked; and I hid myself" (Genesis 3:10). We hide in lists of things to do, people to meet, places to go, phone calls to make, jobs to work, money to earn, bills to pay—all while rehearsing the troubles of our minds. These are just a few of the thorns and thistles, the difficulties and trials that fill life with toil and care. It is written that God cursed the ground for man's sake, not to bring us harm, but that harm might direct us to Him.

The Bible tells us, "For after all these things do the

---

*"Now unto Him that is able to keep you from falling, and to present you faultless before the presence of His glory with exceeding joy, to the only wise God our Savior, be glory and majesty, dominion and power, both now and forever. Amen" (Jude 1:24–25).*

Gentiles seek, for your heavenly Father knoweth that you have need of all these things. But seek ye first the kingdom of God, and His righteousness; and all these things shall be added unto you" (Matthew 6:32–33). God is telling us to walk by faith, not by sight. He's telling us to know the truth that will hold us steady, because when we walk in a storm or the darkness, we can quickly become disoriented and deceived by our senses.

Without clear visibility, our lives wind in circles even while our senses assure us that we're moving straight ahead. When we become disoriented, our senses tell us one thing while the Word of God is saying something else. To stay on the right course, we must rely on the Word that will tell us what is absolutely true, for Jesus Christ said, "[I]t is written, man shall not live by bread alone, but by every word that proceeds out of the mouth of God" (Matthew 4:4). This

---

*"Now unto Him that is able to keep you from falling, and to present you faultless before the presence of His glory with exceeding joy, to the only wise God our Savior, be glory and majesty, dominion and power, both now and forever. Amen" (Jude 1:24–25).*

will provide certainty regardless of how we feel. People who are hurting often say, "I know what is true according to the Word, but I can't feel it right now. Do you know what I mean?" Natural senses in a spiritual storm will cause sin to creep in, and sin fulfilled brings death. But total submission to God will produce the presence, power, witness, and testimony of abundant life in Jesus Christ.

"Be still, and know that I am God: I will be exalted among the heathen, I will be exalted in the earth" (Psalm 46:10). God is telling us not to let a to-do list separate us from His presence, power, and blessing, but to know the truth that will make us free (John 8:32). God bless!

---

*"Now unto Him that is able to keep you from falling, and to present you faultless before the presence of His glory with exceeding joy, to the only wise God our Savior, be glory and majesty, dominion and power, both now and forever. Amen" (Jude 1:24–25).*

# Contents



---

*"Now unto Him that is able to keep you from falling, and to present you faultless before the presence of His glory with exceeding joy, to the only wise God our Savior, be glory and majesty, dominion and power, both now and forever. Amen" (Jude 1:24–25).*

---

*"Now unto Him that is able to keep you from falling, and to present you faultless before the presence of His glory with exceeding joy, to the only wise God our Savior, be glory and majesty, dominion and power, both now and forever. Amen" (Jude 1:24–25).*

# Chapter 1

## Changing of the Attitude

As Jesus spoke to the multitude sitting on the Mount of Olives, He now speaks to you, saying that whoever will come to Him, take hold of His Word, and live according to the Father's purpose shall be blessed. Christ's life ministry reveals God's principles of righteousness, by which you are to live through faith in Him and the power of the indwelling Holy Spirit. Since you have accepted Jesus Christ as Savior and

*"Now unto Him that is able to keep you from falling, and to present you faultless before the presence of His glory with exceeding joy, to the only wise God our Savior, be glory and majesty, dominion and power, both now and forever. Amen" (Jude 1:24–25).*

Lord over your life, God the Father expects to see changes as you obey His Word with the indwelling Holy Spirit.

Becoming a follower of Jesus Christ means turning away from self-centeredness and submitting your life to Christ's direction and control. When Jesus Christ began to teach, He spoke about what is and is not, total obedience, and humble submission to God's will for entering the kingdom. The first thing He taught was how to be blessed, and as you study the Holy Bible, you will see certain requirements for seeking the blessing of God's kingdom. You must be guided by God's ways and values as revealed in Scripture, not by those of the world.

The first steps to being blessed are recognizing that you need the Holy Spirit's power and sustaining grace, and acknowledging your sinfulness and dependence upon God to save and keep you. True humility doesn't mean convincing

---

*"Now unto Him that is able to keep you from falling, and to present you faultless before the presence of His glory with exceeding joy, to the only wise God our Savior, be glory and majesty, dominion and power, both now and forever. Amen" (Jude 1:24–25).*

yourself that you are worthless, but understanding God's perspective on who you are and acknowledging His grace in developing your attitude with this new life upon which you are embarking.

Through the Word of God, Jesus Christ, the apostles, and the Old Testament prophets are teaching you that you cannot develop kingdom values without changing your old ways of thinking and living. As a born-again believer, you cannot mix your old, sinful way of living with your new, righteous way of life in Christ, for then your salvation would be wasted. Selfish ambition can ruin you, but true humility before God will build you into the servant He predestined you to be.

As you study the teachings of the Holy Bible, you will find that God's kingdom is organized differently from worldly kingdoms. In the kingdom of heaven, wealth,

---

*"Now unto Him that is able to keep you from falling, and to present you faultless before the presence of His glory with exceeding joy, to the only wise God our Savior, be glory and majesty, dominion and power, both now and forever. Amen" (Jude 1:24–25).*

power, and authority are unimportant. People of God seek different blessings and benefits, but then God's way usually contradicts the world's way. If you want to live for God, you must be ready to say and do what seems strange to you and the world. You must be willing to give when others take, love when others hate, and help when others abuse. As a believer, your attitude has to be different, enabling you to lay aside your rights in order to serve God and others, even when you are not likely to get recognition for your efforts. Keep your focus, attention, and devotion even more on Christ, and you won't get sidetracked. Know that God will not leave you alone in your struggles to do His will. He will be with you and in you, helping you obey Him and then giving you the power to do it. Hey, let me tell you the secret to a changed life. Shh—listen closely.

Just submit to God's control, and let Him work.

---

*"Now unto Him that is able to keep you from falling, and to present you faultless before the presence of His glory with exceeding joy, to the only wise God our Savior, be glory and majesty, dominion and power, both now and forever. Amen" (Jude 1:24–25).*

Jesus Christ's teachings were not written as a reminder of what He did while here on earth, but as a tool to change your life. This tool—the Word of God—helps you renew your mind, transform your life, convict your soul, clean up your heart, and renew a right spirit in you. God's Word turns your good days into mourning and your radiance into despair, causing you to express deep, heartfelt sorrow over your own weakness in relation to God's standard of righteousness and kingdom power. You're not mourning the death of a loved one, but grieving the things that grieve God and feeling afflicted in your spirit over the sin, immorality, and cruelty manifested in the Church and world. As you weep for the righteous will of God, the Holy Spirit will impress upon you His comfort and power to endure. The Spirit will be with and in you to help and strengthen you, and to teach you the true course of your life. You are being prepared for spiritual

---

*"Now unto Him that is able to keep you from falling, and to present you faultless before the presence of His glory with exceeding joy, to the only wise God our Savior, be glory and majesty, dominion and power, both now and forever. Amen" (Jude 1:24–25).*

warfare, and this war must be carried out with calm faith, humility before God, and hope in His deliverance.

Next is the attitude of meekness. As this becomes a part of your character, you'll tend to commit all of your being to God's righteous way. You will be more concerned about God's work and His people than about what might happen to you personally. The peace of the Lord will envelop you so that you will embrace opposition and submit yourself fully to the will of God, not wanting to gain anything for yourself. You will be able to rest in satisfaction with God's purpose for your life, regardless of any situation that you may come up against.

Stay connected to Christ Jesus and the power of the Holy Spirit, which will cause an even deeper hunger pain that will thirst even to the pit of your soul. You'll experience a deep longing in your heart for God that can be satisfied only by

---

*"Now unto Him that is able to keep you from falling, and to present you faultless before the presence of His glory with exceeding joy, to the only wise God our Savior, be glory and majesty, dominion and power, both now and forever. Amen" (Jude 1:24–25).*

an intimate relationship with Him. The psalmist said, "As the deer panteth after the water brook, so panteth my soul after thee, O God" (Psalm 42:1). Just as water is essential for human life, God and His Word, with the power of the Holy Spirit, are essential for wholeness of life.

When you begin to seek the Lord with all your heart, mind, and soul, He will satisfy your every need and desire according to His will. God's eyes are moving throughout this land, seeking all the hungry, thirsty souls who desire to be satisfied with His presence. Your sense of hunger and thirst is letting you know that your inner person is being transformed, which is marvelous in God's sight. God desires to feed you from the Tree of Life so that you no more snatch fruit from the Tree of the Knowledge of Good and Evil. Seek the Lord, your God, for His mercy endures forever, and when His mercy becomes your mercy, you will be filled with

---

*"Now unto Him that is able to keep you from falling, and to present you faultless before the presence of His glory with exceeding joy, to the only wise God our Savior, be glory and majesty, dominion and power, both now and forever. Amen" (Jude 1:24–25).*

compassion and pity toward those who are suffering from sin or sorrow. Open the way for others to desire to serve the same God you love, praise, worship, and live for. You will deeply desire a forgiving spirit for reconciling differences in your own life and the lives of others.

Remember always that God forgave you and expects you to forgive others their trespasses, for those who serve mercy to others will themselves receive the same. As your attitude changes through obedience to God's will and Word, your eyes will open. You will know that you have been delivered from the power of sin by the grace of God and that you are striving without deceit to please Him and be like Jesus Christ. Only people with unstained and righteous hearts shall see God. And with that, you will develop a pure love for righteousness and a sincere hatred for sin and wickedness. Your ears will be attentive to the voice of God through His

---

*"Now unto Him that is able to keep you from falling, and to present you faultless before the presence of His glory with exceeding joy, to the only wise God our Savior, be glory and majesty, dominion and power, both now and forever. Amen" (Jude 1:24–25).*

Word, and you will greatly desire to walk before God as fair, just, and merciful with humble submission to Him.

Your pure love for God will cause you to praise Him, meditate in the Word, cry out to God, and seek His face with all your heart. As you do these things, God will show Himself to you so that His will can be done, causing you to have peace with Him in Christ Jesus, which is an overwhelming, inexplicable comfort. Walls of separation in your life caused by anger, deception, and lies will be torn down. You will live, walk, and work in peace with all people, both within the church and out in the world, even though you may still face trials, temptations, and criticism for desiring to live in obedience to God's will for your life.

God will make you a witness of His peace in times of trouble and worry. As you pray, God's peace will envelop you day and night, which may feel a bit strange. But don't

---

*"Now unto Him that is able to keep you from falling, and to present you faultless before the presence of His glory with exceeding joy, to the only wise God our Savior, be glory and majesty, dominion and power, both now and forever. Amen" (Jude 1:24–25).*

worry—it's just you becoming a child of God. As you build your new character based on integrity and righteous living, persecutors will try to shake you out of God's perfect plan. But again, don't worry or be afraid—just remember the promises of God's Word, which you have hidden in your heart, and exalt Him because of His worthiness to be praised.

As your faith in God grows, you'll be unpopular at times, but if you believe that Jesus Christ suffered for you in the Garden of Gethsemane, at the whipping post, and on the cross of Calvary, then so shall you suffer for Him. To those who suffer most, God gives His richest blessings. When you face such times, consider how Job, when everything was taken from him, stood on the promises of God even without Jesus Christ and the Holy Spirit. Job lifted up the name of God in praise and thanksgiving, never cursing, denying, or becoming angry with God. Just as Job stood on the promises

---

*"Now unto Him that is able to keep you from falling, and to present you faultless before the presence of His glory with exceeding joy, to the only wise God our Savior, be glory and majesty, dominion and power, both now and forever. Amen" (Jude 1:24–25).*

of God, so should you stand on the foundation of your faith in Christ Jesus during times of persecution, so that you may receive the kingdom and its heavenly rewards.

If you become ashamed of who you are and compromise your godly character to gain status in the eyes of the world or lukewarm believers, then you become useless to God. Jesus said, though not in so many words, that you are like an earthly season with a new taste. Once you begin to walk about in the presence of God's glory, you become a witness giving testimony of God's righteousness, proclaiming in word and deed God's grace and mercy, which is in your Lord and Savior Jesus Christ.

Through you, the world shall taste of the only begotten Son of God, so that anyone who believes in Him receives salvation. You become a light shining in the night, directing people out of their dark places and showing them the way

---

*"Now unto Him that is able to keep you from falling, and to present you faultless before the presence of His glory with exceeding joy, to the only wise God our Savior, be glory and majesty, dominion and power, both now and forever. Amen" (Jude 1:24–25).*

of truth, which will free them and give them the confidence to walk with Christ. Your life, which is being transformed by the Holy Spirit, will be an effective witness to the power of God's Word, and you become a law-abiding citizen of the kingdom of God. Jesus said, "I come not to destroy the law but to fulfill its true purpose" (Matthew 5:17b).

God's commands were written to show you His ways and the works of the kingdom of heaven that must be introduced through you. When you love God with all your being and love others as well, that epiphany reveals the true change in you for the works of God's will through your life. When you listen to the Word of God, it will tell you to be a child who not only hears God's Word, but actually applies it to your life. Hearers change the outcome of the Word, whereas those who apply it perform the divine authority and produce fruit of righteousness through good works. The love of God

---

*"Now unto Him that is able to keep you from falling, and to present you faultless before the presence of His glory with exceeding joy, to the only wise God our Savior, be glory and majesty, dominion and power, both now and forever. Amen" (Jude 1:24–25).*

inside you causes a transformation, and you begin to cover the multitude of sin in and around you by sacrificing your life to God for the freedom of other people.

Keeping God's command and following His Word is a moral code for the expression of Jesus Christ within you. Your faith in Christ is now the fulfilling of the law, by the grace of God and the indwelling Holy Spirit. You must express the love of God in every aspect of your life, such as praying for those who you think are your enemies. That is how you show that Jesus is Lord of your life. Even though you cannot be perfect, aspire to be as much like Christ as possible. Separate yourself from the world's sinful values, and be devoted to God's desires rather than your own, carrying God's love and mercy into the world.

Christ is calling you to excel, rise above mediocrity, and become mature in Him. He calls you to seek the kingdom of

---

*"Now unto Him that is able to keep you from falling, and to present you faultless before the presence of His glory with exceeding joy, to the only wise God our Savior, be glory and majesty, dominion and power, both now and forever. Amen" (Jude 1:24–25).*

God for right living, filling your thoughts with His desires. Take His character for your pattern, and serve and obey Him in everything. If you'll listen to God's Word and obey Christ, you'll build on His solid foundation and weather the storms of life. When life is calm, what you are standing on doesn't matter. But when crisis comes, your foundation is tested, so be sure your life is built on knowing and trusting Jesus Christ. Remember that God will always be with you, wherever you are. He will always guide your footsteps toward Himself, for the power of deliverance comes from Him, not from yourself.

---

*"Now unto Him that is able to keep you from falling, and to present you faultless before the presence of His glory with exceeding joy, to the only wise God our Savior, be glory and majesty, dominion and power, both now and forever. Amen" (Jude 1:24–25).*

## Chapter 2

# Working in Substance Faith

The Bible says that "faith is the substance of things hoped for, the evidence of things not seen ... But without faith it is impossible to please God, for he that come to God must believe that He is, and that He is a rewarder of them that diligently seek Him" (Hebrews 11:1, 6). For faith to produce, you must live with a steadfast trust that God's ways are right with you, a personal loyalty to Jesus Christ as Savior and Lord, and a moral steadfastness to follow Him. You must

---

*"Now unto Him that is able to keep you from falling, and to present you faultless before the presence of His glory with exceeding joy, to the only wise God our Savior, be glory and majesty, dominion and power, both now and forever. Amen" (Jude 1:24–25).*

believe that by trusting God—believing in His provision for your sins and living each day in His power—you can break the cycle of failure in your life.

Take up the shield of faith, for then nothing can hurt you. This faith believes in spiritual realities, leads to righteousness through seeking God, believes in His goodness, has confidence in God's Word, obeys His commands, and regulates life based on the promises of God. The Lord your God approves of a faith that is able to surrender His promises back to Him for fulfillment according to His Will. In God, "this is the victory that overcometh the world, even our faith" (1 John 5:4b). This is a faith that sees eternal realities, experiences the power of God, and loves Jesus Christ to such an extent that the sinful pleasures, worldly values, ungodly ways, and selfish materialism of the world become unimportant, unattractive,

---

*"Now unto Him that is able to keep you from falling, and to present you faultless before the presence of His glory with exceeding joy, to the only wise God our Savior, be glory and majesty, dominion and power, both now and forever. Amen" (Jude 1:24–25).*

and are looked upon with growls of grief. That is when the Will of God becomes your ultimate purpose.

Your faith must go beyond what you believe and become a dynamic part of all you do. True faith will transform your conduct and thoughts. It will reveal the vision that God has for your life and cause an even deeper commitment of your whole self to God. Your faith must express itself in actions. Your trust in God through Christ Jesus produces substance, so that what you cannot see becomes reality. This substance faith will be your unflinching reliance on God in Christ Jesus, taking God at His Word and asking no questions, knowing that all things, whether good or bad, will work out in the best way possible because of your love for God. Then you won't have faith in things, but in God the creator of those things for the purpose of your destiny.

Remember how Abraham was called out from his kindred

---

*"Now unto Him that is able to keep you from falling, and to present you faultless before the presence of His glory with exceeding joy, to the only wise God our Savior, be glory and majesty, dominion and power, both now and forever. Amen" (Jude 1:24–25).*

by God and told to go to a place that he would be shown? He just walked out with what he had, those who were willing to follow him, and his trust in the God who called him to go forth. Abraham died walking toward his faith in God, who promised his descendants a place of rest on the earth. He grew old during his walk with God, never entering the promised land, leaving behind testimony that his faith was counted by God as righteousness.

Having faith in God through Christ Jesus is not about the things He can give you; it's about the God who will fulfill His promises to you. As Abraham was, so shall you be, because you have inside you what he was searching for—Christ and the Holy Spirit of promise, who is able to keep you in all God's ways of righteousness. Just as Abraham walked toward God and His promises by faith, even so God

---

*"Now unto Him that is able to keep you from falling, and to present you faultless before the presence of His glory with exceeding joy, to the only wise God our Savior, be glory and majesty, dominion and power, both now and forever. Amen" (Jude 1:24–25).*

in Christ Jesus desires you to earnestly contend for the faith of the gospel proclaimed by Christ and the apostles.

You must exert yourself to the utmost in defense of God's Word, even though it will be costly and agonizing. Remember that faith is the power of His strength in the presence of His glory, all for your praise and testimony of Him. Faith heals the soul and makes the mute speak, the lame walk, the blind see, and the deaf hear. If you need Jesus to solve a situation, be persistent and don't let anything stop you from getting to Him. That kind of faith is unstoppable, connecting to the power of God and moving mountains. We need faith that's only the size of a mustard seed and trust in God's power to act. This measure of faith will help you change and do what is right, regardless of your past or the disapproval of other people.

Remember that you walk not by appearance, but by faith

---

*"Now unto Him that is able to keep you from falling, and to present you faultless before the presence of His glory with exceeding joy, to the only wise God our Savior, be glory and majesty, dominion and power, both now and forever. Amen" (Jude 1:24–25).*

that is truly in Jesus Christ and produces results, for true faith is a work of God in your heart. Your faith will often be mixed with doubt, but this does not mean that Christ will not respond to your petitions, for the Lord understands and sympathizes with your weakness. You should always confess your lack of faith to the Lord and pray that He will give you the faith that you need. What you receive is not humanly produced; instead, it is a believing faith imparted to your heart by God Himself.

Since true faith is a gift from Christ, it is important that you draw near to Him and His Word. That will deepen your commitment to and confidence in Him, so that you may know Christ personally, as well as knowing His ways, nature, and character as revealed in God's Holy Word. The true knowledge you gain of Christ Jesus involves listening to His Word; following His Spirit; responding to His dealings with

---

*"Now unto Him that is able to keep you from falling, and to present you faultless before the presence of His glory with exceeding joy, to the only wise God our Savior, be glory and majesty, dominion and power, both now and forever. Amen" (Jude 1:24–25).*

you in faith, truth, and obedience; and identifying with His concerns and purposes. In other words you must seek Christ as the author and finisher of your faith (Hebrews 12:2a), knowing that His presence and your obedience to His Word are the source and secret of your faith in Him.

Furthermore, faith is given on the basis of God's wisdom, love, grace, and kingdom purpose to accomplish the will of God and express His love for you. It is not for your own selfish interest, for God will refuse to answer the prayers of anyone who is selfishly ambitious, loves pleasure, and desires honor, power, and riches. As the Bible says, "[T]he just shall live by his faith" (Habakkuk 2:4). This is helpful to all believers who must live through difficult times without seeing signs of hope.

You must always trust that God is directing all things according to His purpose. Your faith in God governs your

---

*"Now unto Him that is able to keep you from falling, and to present you faultless before the presence of His glory with exceeding joy, to the only wise God our Savior, be glory and majesty, dominion and power, both now and forever. Amen" (Jude 1:24–25).*

relationship to Him and your participation in the salvation provided through Jesus Christ. Your faith in the living God brought you to this point, and it will carry you even farther into your future. It is an awesome thing to be admitted into the presence of the mighty God. Your faith in God the Father, the Son, and the Holy Spirit activates your true walk in a righteous life, because it is built by hearing only the Word of God. Just as you received salvation in Christ through faith, so also you grow by faith through His Word.

Keep in mind that your faith is not working alone, but through the power and guidance of the Holy Spirit, who lives in you. Through your faith, He controls your life, engages your attention, molds your habits, and directs your affections. The conviction and confidence of your character are not grounded in your knowledge, but in your testimony, for under every dispensation, you must venture your eternal

---

*"Now unto Him that is able to keep you from falling, and to present you faultless before the presence of His glory with exceeding joy, to the only wise God our Savior, be glory and majesty, dominion and power, both now and forever. Amen" (Jude 1:24–25).*

interests upon the bare Word of God. Only the Holy Spirit can guide your walk and conduct through unseen, eternal realities.

Your hope for heaven, freedom from sin and suffering, and perfect purity and peace result from the perpetual presence of your Savior and Lord, and from all that God in Christ Jesus by the power of the Holy Spirit has done in you—relationships, memories, abilities, family, or material possessions. Use this inventory for prayers of gratitude to increase your thankfulness in the Lord, because thankful people can worship God wholeheartedly. Then gratitude opens your heart to God's peace and enables you to put on true love. As you move forward in this walk, remember the importance of faith:

1) You cannot be saved without faith.
2) You cannot please God without faith.

---

*"Now unto Him that is able to keep you from falling, and to present you faultless before the presence of His glory with exceeding joy, to the only wise God our Savior, be glory and majesty, dominion and power, both now and forever. Amen" (Jude 1:24–25).*

3) You cannot pray without faith.
4) You are to live by faith.
5) You are made righteous by faith.
6) You cannot live victoriously over the world without faith.
7) The Holy Spirit is received by faith.

I hope that your faith broadens your desires in God's will.

---

*"Now unto Him that is able to keep you from falling, and to present you faultless before the presence of His glory with exceeding joy, to the only wise God our Savior, be glory and majesty, dominion and power, both now and forever. Amen" (Jude 1:24–25).*

# Chapter 3

## Seeking and Living the Way of God's Kingdom

The kingdom is more than salvation or the church; it is God expressing Himself with power in all His works. The kingdom is primarily an assertion of divine power in action, present in this world as God's spiritual rule in the hearts of His people. God's kingdom breaking into this world with power involves the deliverance of humanity from the

*"Now unto Him that is able to keep you from falling, and to present you faultless before the presence of His glory with exceeding joy, to the only wise God our Savior, be glory and majesty, dominion and power, both now and forever. Amen" (Jude 1:24–25).*

demonic and sinful, spiritual power over Satan's rule and dominion, and the power to work miracles and heal the sick with the preaching of the gospel. It brings conviction of sin, righteousness, and judgment, but the necessary and fundamental condition of entry into the kingdom of God is to repent and believe the gospel of Jesus Christ.

The gospel of the kingdom has been proclaimed throughout the world, but not everyone is receptive to it. Jesus saves the deepest revelations of Himself for those who love and obey Him. It is your responsibility as a believer to seek unceasingly the kingdom of God in all its manifestations and become zealous for God's presence and power in your life and the Christian community. In Matthew 11:12, even Jesus indicated that the kingdom of heaven is taken hold of only by forceful people committed to breaking away from the sinful and immoral practices of the human race. No

---

*"Now unto Him that is able to keep you from falling, and to present you faultless before the presence of His glory with exceeding joy, to the only wise God our Savior, be glory and majesty, dominion and power, both now and forever. Amen" (Jude 1:24–25).*

matter the cost, such people vigorously seek the kingdom and its power.

Experiencing the kingdom of God and His blessings requires constant exertion and a fight of faith, accompanied by a strong will to resist Satan, sin, and this perverse society. Because you are a true believer in Christ Jesus, it is important for you to take a stand for the Lord. If you just drift along with whatever is pleasant and easy, you will someday discover that you have been worshipping a false god—yourself. But if you are committed to God no matter what, He will show you favor, as He did with Daniel and his three friends. Although they were in a culture that did not honor God, they still obeyed God's laws. When they resolved not to defile themselves, they were being true to a lifelong determination to do what was right and not give in to the pressures around them.

---

*"Now unto Him that is able to keep you from falling, and to present you faultless before the presence of His glory with exceeding joy, to the only wise God our Savior, be glory and majesty, dominion and power, both now and forever. Amen" (Jude 1:24–25).*

You too are often pressured to compromise your standards and live more like the world around you. Merely wanting God's will and way is not enough to stand against the onslaught of temptation; like Daniel, you must resolve to obey God. If you really are true to your Lord and Savior, commit now to your convictions so that when temptations come, you will be ready. As you faithfully follow the Word of God, don't get discouraged when you can't see results. Just keep moving forward and pray, and the fruit of perseverance will grow in your life, along with the promises to believers as they stay attentive to the kingdom's purpose.

Jesus Christ shared many parables about the kingdom of heaven. The Word of God always compels believers to discover the truth, but it conceals the truth from people too lazy or stubborn to see it. As you begin to read and study the words of Jesus Christ as He spoke through the parables,

---

*"Now unto Him that is able to keep you from falling, and to present you faultless before the presence of His glory with exceeding joy, to the only wise God our Savior, be glory and majesty, dominion and power, both now and forever. Amen" (Jude 1:24–25).*

you will surely feel the compelling power of His illustrations, which will help you understand spiritual truth by using everyday objects and relationships.

The Gospels of Matthew, Mark, Luke, and John teach about God and His kingdom, explaining what the kingdom is really like as opposed to your expectations of it. The kingdom is not a geographic location, but a spiritual realm where God rules and believers will share in His eternal life. The kingdom of heaven is more valuable than anything else, and you must be willing to give up everything to obtain it.

The man who found treasure hidden in the field stumbled upon it by accident, but he knew its value when he saw it. The transaction cost him everything, yet he paid nothing for the treasure (Matthew 13:44), which was free with the purchase of the field. So it is with the kingdom of heaven—God gives it to you as a gift, and the price is Jesus Christ's life. The

---

*"Now unto Him that is able to keep you from falling, and to present you faultless before the presence of His glory with exceeding joy, to the only wise God our Savior, be glory and majesty, dominion and power, both now and forever. Amen" (Jude 1:24–25).*

treasure is worth more than gold or silver, and the riches of earth's mines cannot compare with it. This is the treasure found in the Bible, God's great lesson book.

Through the wise counsel of the Holy Spirit, the Bible is God's great educator about the unsearchable riches of Christ Jesus. Many people think that man's wisdom is higher than that of the divine teacher, and they look upon God's lesson book as old-fashioned, stale, and uninteresting, but there are repercussions from neglecting the treasure. When people neglect God, Satan works on their minds, leading them to believe that there is wonderful knowledge to be gained apart from God. He uses deceptive reasoning to lead people to doubt God's Word and replace it with theory that leads to disobedience. Even some God-ordained teachers mingle the sentiments of infidel authors with the education that God has given them, planting in the minds of youth thoughts

---

*"Now unto Him that is able to keep you from falling, and to present you faultless before the presence of His glory with exceeding joy, to the only wise God our Savior, be glory and majesty, dominion and power, both now and forever. Amen" (Jude 1:24–25).*

that will lead to distrust of God and transgression of His law. Little do such teachers realize what will be the result of their work.

Take a look at your children, who will go on to become high school and college students. They may devote their power to acquiring the knowledge that the world has to offer, but unless they truly have knowledge of God and obey His laws that govern their being, they will destroy themselves. By entertaining the wrong ideas, they will lose self-control and be unable to reason correctly about matters that concern them most closely. By acquiring earthly knowledge, they hope to gain a treasure, but by laying down their Bibles, they sacrifice a treasure worth more than anything else.

Search the Word of God until the treasure is in your possession, and educate your children about the truths found there. Many people are content with superficial knowledge,

---

*"Now unto Him that is able to keep you from falling, and to present you faultless before the presence of His glory with exceeding joy, to the only wise God our Savior, be glory and majesty, dominion and power, both now and forever. Amen" (Jude 1:24–25).*

taking for granted that they have all that is essential. Know that Christ is truth and that His Word has deeper significance than appears on the surface. Scripture need not be read by the dim light of tradition or human speculation, but there must be earnest study and close investigation. You cannot expect to gain spiritual knowledge without earnest toil. If you desire to find the treasures of truth, you must dig for them, as the miner digs for the treasure hidden in the earth. No halfhearted, indifferent work will avail.

It is essential for everyone, young and old, to read God's Word and study it with wholehearted earnestness, prayer, and searching for truth as for hidden treasure. If you do this, you will be rewarded, for Christ will quicken your understanding. We have seen only a glimmer of knowledge and wisdom, for we have been working on the surface of the mine, but rich gold is beneath the surface to reward anyone

---

*"Now unto Him that is able to keep you from falling, and to present you faultless before the presence of His glory with exceeding joy, to the only wise God our Savior, be glory and majesty, dominion and power, both now and forever. Amen" (Jude 1:24–25).*

who will dig for it. No one can search the scripture in the spirit of Christ without being rewarded.

If you'll be obedient, you will understand the plan of God's government. In His prayer to the Father, Jesus said, "This is life eternal, that they might know Thee the only true God, and Jesus Christ, whom Thou hast sent" (John 17:3). Knowing God the Father and Jesus Christ the Son imparts power to you by transforming you into the image of God. It gives you mastery over yourself, bringing every impulse and passion of your carnal nature under the control of your Spirit-filled mind. The power of knowing makes you a son or daughter of God and an heir of heaven. It brings you into communion with the mind of the infinite God, and He opens to you the rich treasures of the universe.

As the merchant sought after goodly pearls (Matthew 13:45–46), so has God the Father sought after you, selling

---

*"Now unto Him that is able to keep you from falling, and to present you faultless before the presence of His glory with exceeding joy, to the only wise God our Savior, be glory and majesty, dominion and power, both now and forever. Amen" (Jude 1:24–25).*

everything He had just to purchase you. We are all God's goodly pearls, and through His undying love, He gave His only begotten Son, Jesus Christ, for all the pearls of this world. Think about the pearl, a peculiar gem unlike any other, for it doesn't come from the earth. Pearls aren't shaped by our hands, but by a grain of sand falling inside the shell of a clam. Pearls are not perfectly round, which is how you can tell a real pearl from a fake one.

Just like a pearl, God in Christ Jesus desires you to be peculiar so that He can perform the kingdom of heaven's work in and through you. As a gem of great price, you are to give yourself to Christ and live in willing obedience to His requirements. All that you are—the talents and abilities given to you by Him—are to be consecrated to His service. When you give yourself wholly to Christ, He gives himself and all the treasures of heaven to you. And as you make

---

*"Now unto Him that is able to keep you from falling, and to present you faultless before the presence of His glory with exceeding joy, to the only wise God our Savior, be glory and majesty, dominion and power, both now and forever. Amen" (Jude 1:24–25).*

known the rich treasures of God's grace, you will proclaim, as the apostle Paul said, "What things were gain to me, those I counted loss for Christ. Yea doubtless, and I count all things but loss for the excellency of the knowledge of Christ Jesus my Lord" (Philippians 3:7–8a).

The kingdom of heaven on earth gathers into it both good and evil, but when the mission of the gospel is completed, the judgment will accomplish the work of separation and the destiny of each class will be forever fixed. Though God does not desire the destruction of anyone, yet many will cling to sin and be destroyed.

But God said, "For I know the thoughts that I think toward you ... thoughts of peace, and not of evil, to give you an expected end" to those who truly love and abide in Him (Jeremiah 29:11). That expected end is in Jesus Christ and the salvation plan that He offers to the whole world. His purpose

---

*"Now unto Him that is able to keep you from falling, and to present you faultless before the presence of His glory with exceeding joy, to the only wise God our Savior, be glory and majesty, dominion and power, both now and forever. Amen" (Jude 1:24–25).*

is to restore to you peace and prosperity, an abundance of life with a future of eternal salvation, so what God thinks of you should be of great importance to you. God is always available, and He longs for all men to look to Him and live. Jesus is always open in His loving invitation to anyone who will turn to Him, but a diligent search is necessary.

When you become conscious of your need, sense the satisfying gift of God, and then set out to find Him, be assured of victory as you seek with your whole heart. Everything that God promises in His Word will be yours—cleansing, peace, joy, kindness, gentleness, love, and ultimate victory at the mighty hand of a loving God who delights in bringing you home to His kingdom of eternal peace. The realization of God's promises is delayed by your fault, not by His will. God intends peace, but your conduct is a hindrance, so He graciously waits and suffers long. If you prepare yourself for

---

*"Now unto Him that is able to keep you from falling, and to present you faultless before the presence of His glory with exceeding joy, to the only wise God our Savior, be glory and majesty, dominion and power, both now and forever. Amen" (Jude 1:24–25).*

the accomplishment of God's thoughts, then there will be nothing further to prevent you from enjoying the peace His Word foretells. He is as great in power as He is wise and good in thought.

God has bestowed upon you the noble but perilous faculty of free will, and you cannot measure the limits of this faculty. So you must understand this one thing: God must be found before He can be known and enjoyed, but He is not far from any of us. "For in Him we live, and move, and have our being" (Acts 17:28). You might not recognize God's natural nearness, or it might not be sufficient to bring you into spiritual communion with Him. The God of creation may be "the unknown God" (Acts 17:23), or perhaps you recognize God but don't yet enjoy Him as the portion of your soul. Why? Because sin hides the vision of God and drives the soul into remote spiritual banishment from God, but it

---

*"Now unto Him that is able to keep you from falling, and to present you faultless before the presence of His glory with exceeding joy, to the only wise God our Savior, be glory and majesty, dominion and power, both now and forever. Amen" (Jude 1:24–25).*

does not affect God's physical presence, because He's always there waiting for you to cry out to Him.

God must be searched for, but your search will be successful. You might not find Him at first, or you might not recognize Him in the way you expect, but scripture and experience both testify to the utility and fruitfulness of the soul's search for God. And yes, God does reveal himself to men unexpectedly, as He did to Moses on Horeb, Hagar in the desert, and Gideon threshing wheat by the winepress. However, even such exceptional revelations were made to souls whose habit it was to seek after Him. Nevertheless, before such experience, God draws near to those who do not seek Him, to urge them to search and find Him. The promise of finding God is always attached to conditions that He establishes, for the prodigal must return to the father before being welcomed home.

---

*"Now unto Him that is able to keep you from falling, and to present you faultless before the presence of His glory with exceeding joy, to the only wise God our Savior, be glory and majesty, dominion and power, both now and forever. Amen" (Jude 1:24–25).*

# Chapter 4

# Operating in Kingdom Principles While Facing Worldly Way Conflicts

The Bible says, "[T]here is therefore now no condemnation to them which are in Christ Jesus, who walk not after the flesh, but after the Spirit. For the law of the Spirit of life,

---

*"Now unto Him that is able to keep you from falling, and to present you faultless before the presence of His glory with exceeding joy, to the only wise God our Savior, be glory and majesty, dominion and power, both now and forever. Amen" (Jude 1:24–25).*

in Christ Jesus hath made me free from the law of sin and death" (Romans 8:1–2).

The characteristic principle of the Holy Spirit is to empower you for holy living, whereas the characteristic principle of indwelling sin is to drag you down to death. The law of gravity says that when you throw a ball into the air, it comes back down because it is heavier than the air it displaces. But in the believer, the law of life overcomes the law of gravity because the Holy Spirit supplies the risen life of the Lord Jesus, freeing the believer from the law of sin and death, though not freeing you to do whatever you want, for that would lead you back into slavery to your selfish desires. When you hold in your hands a living bird, which is heavier than the air it displaces, it is held unto death, but when you toss it into the air, it flies away because the law of life in the bird overcomes the law of gravity.

---

*"Now unto Him that is able to keep you from falling, and to present you faultless before the presence of His glory with exceeding joy, to the only wise God our Savior, be glory and majesty, dominion and power, both now and forever. Amen" (Jude 1:24–25).*

Thanks to Christ, you are now able to live unselfishly, which was previously impossible, because the character and work of a true believer in Christ now exemplifies your strength. You have received the ministry of mercy without failing; you are not disheartened, but have become courageous in your strength of conviction and principles. You are thoroughly cleansed of the things of dishonesty and shame, such as falsehood, unchastity, meanness, and selfishness, for every sin is shameful and makes the conscience blush.

You are also identified by your straightforwardness, sincerity, and honesty, and you speak the truth about Jesus Christ in a plain, understandable manner. Also live it out in your life before others, so that they may see the truth through your example. With your life, appeal to the conscience of humanity through the truth under the inspection of Almighty God. Always remember and acknowledge that

---

*"Now unto Him that is able to keep you from falling, and to present you faultless before the presence of His glory with exceeding joy, to the only wise God our Savior, be glory and majesty, dominion and power, both now and forever. Amen" (Jude 1:24–25).*

the Holy Spirit of God is leading, guiding, and directing your way of life, for the Bible says, "This I say then, Walk in the Spirit, and you shall not fulfill the lust of the flesh" (Galatians 5:16).

It is not enough that you begin the divine life; you must maintain it through all its stages and experiences. Your works are effectual only by the Spirit, and your life must be in harmony with the mind of the Spirit. His will must be your constant guide, which implies a full surrender to His authority and guidance. The Spirit's guidance will keep you apart from all sinful indulgences, worldliness, and the sins and purposes of the merely natural man. You shall not trust in your own strength, and so you shall be kept; you shall consult His will supremely, and He will deliver you from the perversities and delusions of your own will.

Indwelling sin is the calamity of all the people of God,

---

*"Now unto Him that is able to keep you from falling, and to present you faultless before the presence of His glory with exceeding joy, to the only wise God our Savior, be glory and majesty, dominion and power, both now and forever. Amen" (Jude 1:24–25).*

but there are two powers at work within us: "The flesh lust against the Spirit, and the Spirit against the flesh" (Galatians 5:17a). Sin uses the senses to mar the Spirit's power, as the flesh presents to the eyes ungodly temptations of every sort to inflame evil passions, and it finds the tongue often too ready to serve its purpose. The Spirit, however, is entrenched within the soul and will not be dislodged. He too uses the senses, the hands and feet, for the purpose of edification.

These two natures abide in one vessel, forever struggling for the soul of man, and this struggle keeps you from accomplishing all righteousness. You fail at achieving freedom from temptation, living an uninterrupted life with God, and becoming perfect as God is perfect. God's will is for the conflicts within you to humble you by giving you a better understanding of your sin. God's will is for you to

---

*"Now unto Him that is able to keep you from falling, and to present you faultless before the presence of His glory with exceeding joy, to the only wise God our Savior, be glory and majesty, dominion and power, both now and forever. Amen" (Jude 1:24–25).*

become more watchful and attentive to who He is in you, and for you to long more deeply for His grace and nature.

Regarding knowledge, being led by the Holy Spirit involves the desire to hear, the readiness to obey God's Word, and the sensitivity to discern between your feelings and His promptings. "Where the Spirit of the Lord is, there is liberty," for "Christ is the end of the Law for righteousness to everyone that believeth" (2 Corinthians 3:17b, Romans 10:4). As long as you continually believe God in Jesus Christ, your freedom is forever sealed in heaven, where all the spiritual blessing are in Him and with Him. God didn't choose you because you deserved it. No, God is gracious and freely gives His grace and loving favor to those He saves. No religious or moral effort can gain it, for it comes only from God's mercy and love.

At times, you will face persecution, illness, various forms

---

*"Now unto Him that is able to keep you from falling, and to present you faultless before the presence of His glory with exceeding joy, to the only wise God our Savior, be glory and majesty, dominion and power, both now and forever. Amen" (Jude 1:24–25).*

of imprisonment, and even death, and these hardships will make you fear that you have been abandoned by Christ. But you can overcome that fear by trusting the Lord with all your heart and mind. The Bible says, "There is nothing that can separate you from the Love of God in Christ Jesus" (Romans 8:39). If you continually believe in Christ, you are a super-conqueror, and His love will protect you from all such forces.

Therefore, your walk must be worthy of His call in you, showing that your faith is not a sham or deception, but a great reality. A life worthy of God in Christ Jesus will appeal to the heart and head of anyone watching, demonstrating that your belief in Christ is not only a reality, but also a great obligation and blessing. When frustration and conflict rains down on your life, hold fast to your faith in Christ Jesus, that it may appeal to the conscience of other people and compel them to say, "That is what we ought to be." Yes, you must be a model

---

*"Now unto Him that is able to keep you from falling, and to present you faultless before the presence of His glory with exceeding joy, to the only wise God our Savior, be glory and majesty, dominion and power, both now and forever. Amen" (Jude 1:24–25).*

for others, because human nature desires something on its own level—something visible and tangible, like a stepping-stone between Christ and themselves. People sneer at model Christians, but not at model soldiers or servants.

If you are the Christian that you proclaim to be, aim at staying as close to Christ as possible. It's a hard task, but follow the mark with resolve. Walk in a worthy manner, consistent with a Christian's dignified position as a member of the Body of Christ. That is a walk, with God's help, within the reach of everyone—a walk of holiness, humility, forbearance, forgiveness, patience, and charity. You must seek to make the world brighter and better, urged to do so by the sin, misery, and danger regarding the soul.

Your victories will often be gained through meekness and endurance. In this Christian life, you will fight against the powerful evil forces of fallen angels directed by Satan,

---

*"Now unto Him that is able to keep you from falling, and to present you faultless before the presence of His glory with exceeding joy, to the only wise God our Savior, be glory and majesty, dominion and power, both now and forever. Amen" (Jude 1:24–25).*

a vicious fighter. In this walk, remember this saying: Lions attack sick, young or straggling animals, they choose victims who are alone and not alert. But instead of a lion, it will be Satan coming to devour you. To withstand his attack, you must depend on God and use every piece of His armor, keeping your eyes on Christ. James 4:7 says, "Resist the devil, and he will flee from you."

Even for ordinary purposes, you have to fight against idleness, lust, dishonest tendencies, and many other things in yourself—opposition, ill treatment, being tempted by others, and the depressing effects of trials and disappointments. It's hard work to fight monotony, weariness, and a longing for ease, and when you're sick or depressed, it is often hard to hold on to the straight path of hard duty and turn away from the allurements of pleasure. The life of a Christian is even more of a battle, because the chief enemies are unseen,

---

*"Now unto Him that is able to keep you from falling, and to present you faultless before the presence of His glory with exceeding joy, to the only wise God our Savior, be glory and majesty, dominion and power, both now and forever. Amen" (Jude 1:24–25).*

and sometimes it will seem like an aimless, careless life. But Christ said, "If any man will come after me, let him deny himself, take up his cross and follow me" (Luke 9:23). As a Christian, walk worthy of the vocation to which you are called.

In the Old Testament, God tells Joshua, "Only be very strong and courageous" (Joshua 1:7a). This strength is needed because of the burdens, conflicts, and temptations of life. To respond to life's sorrows and cares, Christians must have strength of heart, strength of purpose, and strength of will. You must grow in Christ toward that condition in which you shall be without spot or wrinkle, advancing in spite of hosts of spiritual foes, which is no easy task. Though it may seem strange to be exposed to such enemies, consider the source of your strength. The strength poured into you is the strength

---

*"Now unto Him that is able to keep you from falling, and to present you faultless before the presence of His glory with exceeding joy, to the only wise God our Savior, be glory and majesty, dominion and power, both now and forever. Amen" (Jude 1:24–25).*

of Christ springing out of your realization of the continued presence, love, and help of the Redeemer.

The Lord is continually exhorting His people to be strong, because without strength, determination, and energy, your elaborate thinking and beautiful sentiments are worthless. You may believe intellectually, but if you are too weak to act according to your belief, then it counts for nothing, for it is your duty to be strong in the Lord. Strength in the Lord comes from divine inspiration; you cannot be strong by merely willing to be so. The body must gain strength through a nourishing diet, bracing air, and exercise. Spiritual strength arises from feeding upon Christ and His Word in faith and by prayer, and you must be in Christ Jesus to have this strength. The closer your union to Christ becomes, the more vigorously you will be supplied with His strength. "It is God that gird you with strength, and make your way

---

*"Now unto Him that is able to keep you from falling, and to present you faultless before the presence of His glory with exceeding joy, to the only wise God our Savior, be glory and majesty, dominion and power, both now and forever. Amen" (Jude 1:24–25).*

perfect" (Psalm 18:32). God doesn't promise to eliminate challenges; instead, He gives you His strength to meet those challenges head-on. If this walk was not complicated, you would not grow. When your faith may be struggling or weak, accept His provisions and care for you, for His strength is your source of strength.

Everything that you hear and learn of God in Christ Jesus is vital to your becoming a peculiar person in Christ. He must be magnified not only in your body, labors, and suffering, but also in your spirit. You must live in the spirit of the Savior's words, not thinking about how to preserve the life you're living, but pressing toward God and His kingdom with all your heart so that He may keep you for eternity. You must die to the world, but live to God.

But you must know by your own experiences the power of Christ dwelling in your soul before you can feel that

---

*"Now unto Him that is able to keep you from falling, and to present you faultless before the presence of His glory with exceeding joy, to the only wise God our Savior, be glory and majesty, dominion and power, both now and forever. Amen" (Jude 1:24–25).*

death is truly gained. Your sins died with Him, and you are no longer condemned; you have become one with Christ, and His experiences are now yours as well. In unity with Christ, you died to your old life, and now you must regularly crucify sinful desires that will try to keep you from following Him. Yet the focus of your new life is not on dying, but on living. You have been crucified with Christ, so you have also been raised with Him, reconciled to God, and made free to grow in His likeness. Now you have Jesus Christ in your heart, the "Mystery which has been hid from ages and from generations" (Colossians 1:26).

Ground yourself in His Word, learn daily about the Savior, develop your spiritual knowledge, and press toward His wisdom. Pray for understanding; God has given you a mind for learning, so never stop using it. The key to your saved life is to center on Christ, continually following His

---

*"Now unto Him that is able to keep you from falling, and to present you faultless before the presence of His glory with exceeding joy, to the only wise God our Savior, be glory and majesty, dominion and power, both now and forever. Amen" (Jude 1:24–25).*

leadership by being rooted, built up, and established in the faith. Every day, the Lord desires to guide you and help with your problems. You have the ability to live for Christ by committing your life and submitting your will to Him. Seek to learn from Him, His life, and His teachings, and always recognize the Holy Spirit's power in you.

By accepting Christ and regarding your old nature as dead, you change your moral and ethical behavior by letting Christ live within you, so that He can shape you into what you should be in Him. Jesus Christ wants to clean you of sexual and verbal sin, gossip, rage, and backbiting so that you can witness to the world like a lighthouse on a stormy night, displaying love, faith, and hope. Imitate Christ's merciful, forgiving attitude, and let love guide your life. Let the peace of God rule in your heart, always be thankful, keep His word in you at all times, and live as Jesus Christ's representative.

---

*"Now unto Him that is able to keep you from falling, and to present you faultless before the presence of His glory with exceeding joy, to the only wise God our Savior, be glory and majesty, dominion and power, both now and forever. Amen" (Jude 1:24–25).*

And in these troubled times, realize that God's infinite love and forgiveness can help you love and forgive other people. Let God worry about the wrongs you've suffered; don't quench your life with bitter feuding, but live renewed in love and joy. Know that you are called to assume the new habits of Christian grace and goodness—what the Divine Father is, has done for you, and intends you to be. Become sensible of your filial relationship to Him, loyally embracing His Will and seeking to be conformed to His nature as that is translated for you into the image of His Son, for then you shall be holy in all manner of conversation.

In the spirit of this love, peculiar Christians possess their souls in patience through all the strenuous endeavors, painful collisions, and vexing wrongs of life. They wear the girdle of perfection and attain the perfect Christian temper, though their faith and hope are assailed by many enemies, whether

---

*"Now unto Him that is able to keep you from falling, and to present you faultless before the presence of His glory with exceeding joy, to the only wise God our Savior, be glory and majesty, dominion and power, both now and forever. Amen" (Jude 1:24–25).*

among the common incidents of life or in the heavenly places of their richest experiences and most exalted communion with spiritual things. Sometimes strange influences shadow their inner lives, coming from they know not where or how. Sometimes the ruggedness and gloom of their paths create mental perplexities and a chilling, confused intellectual atmosphere around them. In any or all of these ways, a trial of faith comes to everyone who has a faith worth trials.

---

*"Now unto Him that is able to keep you from falling, and to present you faultless before the presence of His glory with exceeding joy, to the only wise God our Savior, be glory and majesty, dominion and power, both now and forever. Amen" (Jude 1:24–25).*

# Chapter 5

# The Way of Holding On Until the End

"And take heed to yourselves, lest at any time your hearts be overcharged with surfeiting and drunkenness, and cares of this life, and so that day come upon you unawares. For as a snare shall it come on all them that dwell on the face of the whole earth. Watch ye therefore, and pray always, that ye may be accounted worthy to escape all these things that

---

*"Now unto Him that is able to keep you from falling, and to present you faultless before the presence of His glory with exceeding joy, to the only wise God our Savior, be glory and majesty, dominion and power, both now and forever. Amen" (Jude 1:24–25).*

shall come to pass, and to stand before the Son of man" (Luke 21:34–36).

When the way grows dark, you must not yield to an unspiritual anxiety but rise to a holy, childlike faith in your heavenly Father. Be attentive in your wait, and watch with prayer and supplication to the Lord Jesus Christ, for you have heard that His return will be at an hour and day unknown to either Christ or man. Your job in this life is to stand firm in His Word and will, so that you may be accounted worthy before the Son of Man for the relationship you have voluntarily sustained with Him; how you received His invitation; with what fullness you accepted Him as your redeemer, friend, and Lord of your heart and life; how you have served Him since you called yourself by His name; how closely you have followed Him; how obedient you have been to His commandments; and how earnest and faithful you

---

*"Now unto Him that is able to keep you from falling, and to present you faultless before the presence of His glory with exceeding joy, to the only wise God our Savior, be glory and majesty, dominion and power, both now and forever. Amen" (Jude 1:24–25).*

have showed yourself in His cause. The Lord wants you to be totally conformed to His image and redeemed from all iniquity and sin, with purity of heart and a loving spirit of unselfishness, devotion, generosity, and tender care. Jesus is coming to find you spotless and without wrinkles, clean on both the inside and the outside.

God chose you from the foundation of the world to be holy in Him. Jesus Christ came to earth and gave Himself as a selfless sacrifice to redeem you from your sins. The Holy Spirit was sent to empower, keep, lead, guide, counsel, sanctify, and remind you through the Word of Truth about the grace and mercy of God's love and salvation through Jesus Christ. God desires obedience and a right heart, without empty compliances to the sacrifice system. His new and living way for you to please Him is not by keeping laws or even by abstaining from sin, but by coming to Him in faith

---

*"Now unto Him that is able to keep you from falling, and to present you faultless before the presence of His glory with exceeding joy, to the only wise God our Savior, be glory and majesty, dominion and power, both now and forever. Amen" (Jude 1:24–25).*

to be forgiven and then following Him in loving obedience. The imminent return of Christ should motivate you to live with and for Him. You should ask yourself the question: Am I really ready to meet Christ?

Unlike the gods of Rome and pagan cults, Christ is not adulterous, spiteful, bloodthirsty, or promiscuous. But your Holy God does expect you to imitate Him by following His high moral standards, so like Him, you should be merciful and just, sacrificing yourself for others. The Lord your God also desires you to be holy in everything you do, which means being devoted and dedicated to Him, set aside for His special use, and set apart from sin and its influences. You cannot become holy on your own, but the Lord Jesus gives you His Holy Spirit to help you obey and to give you power to overcome sin and Satan. God wants to deliver the

---

*"Now unto Him that is able to keep you from falling, and to present you faultless before the presence of His glory with exceeding joy, to the only wise God our Savior, be glory and majesty, dominion and power, both now and forever. Amen" (Jude 1:24–25).*

world of all evil, but He wants you and all others called by His Name to live a life that's pleasing to Him.

Christ's return is sure to break forth. He shall sound the trumpet, and everyone who died in Him will rise to Him, and those who are still alive in Him shall be caught up in the sky with Him and the rest of the saints to enter into His heavenly kingdom. So you must adhere to the instructions that God has given you and be prepared, for no one truly knows when the Lord will return and that great day of God's judgment will begin. Be watchful, so that you won't be caught unprepared. Be an armed sentinel and guard yourself against surprise.

Be faithful to Christ and love all men, which will preserve your heart against evil influences, and the hope of your salvation will defend you against being seduced by the world's pleasures or honors. Forgiveness of enemies is

---

*"Now unto Him that is able to keep you from falling, and to present you faultless before the presence of His glory with exceeding joy, to the only wise God our Savior, be glory and majesty, dominion and power, both now and forever. Amen" (Jude 1:24–25).*

a Christian virtue, and it must be free, full, and universal. Don't allow feelings of enmity or ill will toward your fellow men to lodge in your heart. Be full of joy, and live by your faith in Christ, diligent in the performance of your religious duties.

Pray with a constant intercourse between God and your soul; your prayers should be like Jacob's dream about angels continually ascending the mystic ladder to the throne of God. Be sure that you do not quench the Holy Spirit by indulging in sensuality, covetousness, pride, formality, or a lukewarm approach to your Christian walk. You are a child of the light and the day, so exercise vigilance and sobriety in view of the command before you. Do not sleep as other people do, for sleep and drunkenness are the works of darkness done in the night. When you're spiritually asleep, you sleep through life's agitations beneath the thunder and pleadings of mercy

---

*"Now unto Him that is able to keep you from falling, and to present you faultless before the presence of His glory with exceeding joy, to the only wise God our Savior, be glory and majesty, dominion and power, both now and forever. Amen" (Jude 1:24–25).*

from the cross. Like a drunkard, you are intoxicated with life's delights, minding earthly things, and occupied with the unfruitful works of darkness.

But that's not you, for you are a good soldier bound to endure hardness, going forth into the conflicts of life equipped with divine armor—not to commit aggression, but for the defense of the aggressor. By the Word of God, you are to conquer the works of darkness, for God did not appoint you to die, but to obtain His salvation. Hold tight to your call and know that your security as a believer depends not upon yourself, but upon God's unchangeable and loving purpose for your life.

What you have does not gain precedence over your existence except in the word of God, knowing that your life is too great a thing—too divine a gift—to be supported wholly by outward things. Knowing is the key to holding on,

---

*"Now unto Him that is able to keep you from falling, and to present you faultless before the presence of His glory with exceeding joy, to the only wise God our Savior, be glory and majesty, dominion and power, both now and forever. Amen" (Jude 1:24–25).*

for the word spoken out of God's mouth is the food for your soul and the stay of your heart. Because His word is living and powerful, it lives and abides forever. He has written your path's purpose along with all that you shall go through, and those situations and circumstances, good and bad, will mold and shape you into the image God has planned for you.

Jesus Christ understands your battle with evil, because He fought a similar battle, from His fast in the wilderness to the cross at Calvary. As you live for Jesus, you will experience troubles and hardship, because you're trying to be God's servant in a perverse world. Some people claim that troubles result from sin and lack of faith, but when your life is committed to the Lord, your troubles become part of His plan for your purpose in Jesus Christ. That is also an indication that you are taking a stand for your faith in God's

---

*"Now unto Him that is able to keep you from falling, and to present you faultless before the presence of His glory with exceeding joy, to the only wise God our Savior, be glory and majesty, dominion and power, both now and forever. Amen" (Jude 1:24–25).*

will. That doesn't mean that you're perfect, but that you are on the path to perfection in Christ.

In this life, you'll be surrounded by many influences tending to lead you into error, delusion, skepticism, and infidelity. The truth in God's Word should be the great subject of your inquiry, so pursue it to wherever it leads in Christ, so that you aren't susceptible to the condemnation of people who don't believe the truth and take pleasure in unrighteousness.

Life is not a script that you meaninglessly act out; instead, it is a time of deciding whether you will live for God. The Lord God will examine what kind of worker you have been for Him, so build your life on His word and build His word into your life. If you spend your time ignoring God's word, you will be ashamed at the judgment. Let the path to which God has called you be an encouragement to stand with your

---

*"Now unto Him that is able to keep you from falling, and to present you faultless before the presence of His glory with exceeding joy, to the only wise God our Savior, be glory and majesty, dominion and power, both now and forever. Amen" (Jude 1:24–25).*

Lord and Master for the advancement of the gospel. Preach it, vindicate it, uphold it against all gainsayers, adorn it with your own life as did Jesus Christ, and exert your utmost effort to its maintenance and triumph. Let God use you as an instrument of His will.

A time is coming when Christians will hardly know which way to turn or what to do. You will have to live under a constant sense of hindrance and difficulty of one sort or another. It will be tempting to love pleasure more than God, and if you're not possessed by the truth, error will easily defeat you. As a person called by God, you must contend for your faith in Christ and not let the truth of the Bible be compromised, because it gives you the real facts about Jesus and salvation. When that time comes, you must—without a shadow of doubt—believe, trust, and know that the Bible is the inspired Word of God. When the scripture is twisted

---

*"Now unto Him that is able to keep you from falling, and to present you faultless before the presence of His glory with exceeding joy, to the only wise God our Savior, be glory and majesty, dominion and power, both now and forever. Amen" (Jude 1:24–25).*

and manipulated, people will become confused over right and wrong, and they'll lose sight of the only path that leads to eternal life in Jesus Christ.

The character of evil men is evident in the world and the revelation of God's word. An atmosphere of selfishness will be created by people who exclude God from the central place to which He is entitled in their lives. They will believe lies that will reinforce their own selfish beliefs, and they'll become arrogantly boastful, full of pride and contempt toward others. They will be disobedient, wandering about without direction or guidance, lawlessly driven, unthankful, impatient with being ruled by their parents. Those who were allowed to have their own way in early life will grow up not showing gratitude to their parents or even in the ordinary exchanges of life, nor will they show respect to God for His mercies. Some will even be members of the church of

---

*"Now unto Him that is able to keep you from falling, and to present you faultless before the presence of His glory with exceeding joy, to the only wise God our Savior, be glory and majesty, dominion and power, both now and forever. Amen" (Jude 1:24–25).*

Jesus Christ, exhibiting a form of godliness but denying its power. They'll resist the truth of God's word because of its all-discovering, all-judging power. With minds rotten to the core, they'll be reprobate concerning the faith of Jesus Christ.

In the wake of this wicked atmosphere, confusion will result from seductive hostile spirits giving rise to soul-destroying doctrines, for you will not be wrestling against flesh and blood in those despicable moments. Many souls will be drawn away from the truth and follow these seducers with their false doctrine. People dislike strict lives, so they will be easily led to embrace systems that offer some new phase of error or permit lax morals. Therefore you must cultivate the gift that was given you by God in the Holy Spirit at your conversion, because to stand against this wild adversary, you will need the power of God.

---

*"Now unto Him that is able to keep you from falling, and to present you faultless before the presence of His glory with exceeding joy, to the only wise God our Savior, be glory and majesty, dominion and power, both now and forever. Amen" (Jude 1:24–25).*

Now your faith must go beyond what you believe and become a dynamic part of all you do—a hope to the end; an armed worrier, grave and calm, ready for conflict because of assured victory. Your faith will be as wings to lift you above care and sorrows, and as cords to bind you to duty and toil. Your Christian virtue will require determined effort. You will need to create opportunities where you cannot find them and work at times both convenient and inconvenient. Exercise your patience and use all the resources of a sanctified understanding, that you may encourage others to keep to the ways of good doctrine and holiness.

Much like Stephen, the first martyr in the New Testament book of Acts, you should always be ready to expound with resolve the gospel of Jesus Christ, which will indicate your profound seriousness of purpose and spirit. Remember that obedience is much better than sacrifice. Obey your leaders

---

*"Now unto Him that is able to keep you from falling, and to present you faultless before the presence of His glory with exceeding joy, to the only wise God our Savior, be glory and majesty, dominion and power, both now and forever. Amen" (Jude 1:24–25).*

who are walking in the righteousness of God's will, but be sure to keep your eyes on Christ, your ultimate leader. He will not change in the face of a changing society, so submit to the will of God and serve only Him, not mammon.

Clothe yourself with humility, so that you may enjoy His grace. Make the blood of Jesus Christ your only plea, and surrender your heart to the powerful operation of the Holy Spirit. When you submit to the righteousness of God in His gospel, you shall then reverence, admire, and obey His moral laws. You will allow Him to control you in body and mind; intellect and conscience; heart, will, action, and habit, as you long and labor to be holy. Be content with the life to which God has assigned you, bear afflictions patiently, and in times of sorrow, don't challenge God's sovereignty or distrust His love, but always rejoice in your tribulations.

Peculiar believers in Jesus Christ will emphasize faith

---

*"Now unto Him that is able to keep you from falling, and to present you faultless before the presence of His glory with exceeding joy, to the only wise God our Savior, be glory and majesty, dominion and power, both now and forever. Amen" (Jude 1:24–25).*

in action, and right living will be the evidence and result of their faith. They will serve with compassion, love, and truth, living in obedience to God's commands with true love toward others. As citizens of the kingdom of heaven on earth, they will draw others to Christ through their love for God and His will. Therefore I pray that the Holy Spirit will fill you with all the resources of His character that you need for your life's victories. In Jesus Christ's name, amen and amen.

I believe that from time to time, we all need extra help or encouragement to push us to the next level of trust and commitment to Christ Jesus our Lord and King. So I have decided to add one of the sermons that I have preached, as the Lord has led me to at certain seasons, to the congregation of Love Thy Neighbor Ministry. During a season of misconception, the Lord gave me this message: "Have you

---

*"Now unto Him that is able to keep you from falling, and to present you faultless before the presence of His glory with exceeding joy, to the only wise God our Savior, be glory and majesty, dominion and power, both now and forever. Amen" (Jude 1:24–25).*

really considered the cost of following Jesus Christ?" (Luke 14:25–35).

This passage tells us that we must be so committed to living for Jesus that we hate everything else by comparison, even our own life. We shouldn't actually long to die or be careless or destructive with the life that God through Jesus Christ has given us, nor should we hate or despise our family. But we should be willing to die if doing so will glorify Christ, and to stand for and with Christ even if our family wants nothing to do with Him.

Have you really considered the cost of following Jesus Christ? What room is there in your walk with Jesus Christ for calculation? What amount of reckoning before acting is permissible to you as a follower of Jesus Christ? When and in what way should you ask of yourself, "Can I afford to do this?" or "Have I strength enough to undertake this calling?"

---

*"Now unto Him that is able to keep you from falling, and to present you faultless before the presence of His glory with exceeding joy, to the only wise God our Savior, be glory and majesty, dominion and power, both now and forever. Amen" (Jude 1:24–25).*

Verse 25 tells us that these people were following Jesus because they were fascinated by His presence and awestruck by His teachings, and they marveled at His mighty works. But they were far from entering into His Spirit or sharing His high purpose, so they needed to understand what discipleship to Jesus meant and what absolute self-surrender it involved. Jesus did not come to bring peace into your life, but division and separation from all that you've ever known or been interested in, such as your friends and loved ones, and wants and selfish desires.

In verse 26, Jesus is not encouraging disobedience to parents or separation from spouses, nor is He saying to abandon your children, sisters, and brothers. Instead, He is telling us that His presence demands a decision. Nothing less than the first place in your heart must be offered to Jesus, and all relations must be put below Him.

---

*"Now unto Him that is able to keep you from falling, and to present you faultless before the presence of His glory with exceeding joy, to the only wise God our Savior, be glory and majesty, dominion and power, both now and forever. Amen" (Jude 1:24–25).*

The unity of marriage illustrates the intensity of Christ's love; the husband owes much to the wife, and the wife to the husband. The marriage union is close and intimate, but Jesus Christ comes closer to our hearts than husband or wife, so He should be nearer and dearer. Children are considered a gift from God, but even they come second in our hearts after Jesus.

Jesus tells us this because it is much better to know what you are doing by following Him than to start something that you later feel obliged to abandon, or to take on a duty to which you later find yourself unequal. He knows that some people will follow Him and others won't, but conflict will inevitably arise.

Verse 27 says that taking up your cross and following Jesus means being willing to publicly identify with Him, experience certain opposition, and face suffering and even

---

*"Now unto Him that is able to keep you from falling, and to present you faultless before the presence of His glory with exceeding joy, to the only wise God our Savior, be glory and majesty, dominion and power, both now and forever. Amen" (Jude 1:24–25).*

death for His sake. It means understanding that you belong to Jesus and live to serve His purpose. Jesus wants you to think through your enthusiasm for Him and decide whether what you are feeling is real. He's encouraging you to either go deeper in understanding the mission or turn back, because following Him requires total submission.

Verses 28–30 tell us that before wise people commit themselves to any policy, they carefully consider whether they can carry it through. Every wise builder calculates the cost before he begins to build; otherwise the building might be left incomplete if there is not enough money to complete it. Following Christ is not something to take up on a trial basis. Salvation in Christ calls for an ultimate commitment.

Verses 31–33 tell us that the wise king always estimates his military strength before declaring war. Have you thought about whether you are prepared to make a full surrender

---

*"Now unto Him that is able to keep you from falling, and to present you faultless before the presence of His glory with exceeding joy, to the only wise God our Savior, be glory and majesty, dominion and power, both now and forever. Amen" (Jude 1:24–25).*

of your will to Christ's will and your life to His service? Following Christ may cause you to lose social status, and you may even have to give up control of your money, time, and career. Consider the matter at hand, and weigh everything before you act. Count the cost, and decide with a full understanding of what you are getting yourself into.

In Matthew 5:13, Jesus Christ says that you are the salt of the earth, but salt can lose its flavor when it gets wet and then dries. When exposed to sun and rain, salt may lose its virtue while retaining its appearance. "Having a form of godliness, but denying the power thereof" (2 Timothy 3:5). It is a shame that many Christians blend into the world and avoid the cost of standing for Christ. Some may use Christian speech in their conversations, and yet the doctrine they declare may be weakened and ineffective. Their faith has lost its excellence and virtue, becoming blurred and

---

*"Now unto Him that is able to keep you from falling, and to present you faultless before the presence of His glory with exceeding joy, to the only wise God our Savior, be glory and majesty, dominion and power, both now and forever. Amen" (Jude 1:24–25).*

blemished, spotted and stained. Their lives contain nothing beyond conventional standards and behavior or morals—not animated by the love of Christ, filled with the Spirit of God, or governed by the principles of Christ. Jesus says that when believers lose their distinctive flavor, they become worthless to the kingdom.

But that won't happen with you, because you, as one of Christ's saints, are all in. You've made an eternal commitment, for the journey does not stop here. It is ongoing even until the coming of Christ, so stay strong and sure to the call of God in Christ. "So be strong in the power of His might" (Ephesians 6:10). And be blessed! Amen.

---

*"Now unto Him that is able to keep you from falling, and to present you faultless before the presence of His glory with exceeding joy, to the only wise God our Savior, be glory and majesty, dominion and power, both now and forever. Amen" (Jude 1:24–25).*

CPSIA information can be obtained
at www.ICGtesting.com
Printed in the USA
BVHW071021250820
587150BV00002B/145

9 781973 696568